¡ Infórm...

Jean and David We...

JKSimpson

23

Longman

Acknowledgements

The authors gratefully acknowledge the help they have received from

Joyce and Phil Clarke
Jo Daly
Jenny Kelly
Jane O'Donnell

The would especially like to thank Trinidad Martínez de Ventura for all her continuing support, advice and encouragement.

Photographs by

Jo Daly, pages 7, 11, 26
Jane O'Donnell, pages 10, 11, 12, 24, 54
Jean Webb, pages 10, 75

By the same authors
Aprobado
In your own words: Spanish

LONGMAN GROUP UK LIMITED
Longman House
Burnt Mill, Harlow, Essex CM20 2JE, England
and Associated Companies throughout the World

First published 1989
Third impression 1994
ISBN 0 582 00643 0

Set in 10/12 pt Helvetica (Linotron)

Printed in China
PPC/03

Contents

Preface

¡Infórmate! aims to provide lively, authentic reading material for students working towards basic level GCSE. The materials included and the tasks set are of the kind that may be encountered when visiting Spain or when preparing for such a visit (e.g. understanding letters, prospectuses, brochures).

The book comprises an introduction, *Reading Spanish*, designed to increase students' awareness of strategies for reading comprehension, and eight sections, each based on a topic. While the earlier sections are in general easier than those at the end of the book, there is no rigid incline of difficulty: it is anticipated that teachers will wish to deal with topics as and when they arise in their normal teaching programme rather than working straight through the book. Within each section, however, items are graded according to difficulty.

In addition, the authors hope that ¡Infórmate! may help overcome the problems faced by teachers working with groups of varied ability. As well as being used as part of a regular course, it might also provide reinforcement for students who, for whatever reason, need extra stimulus and practice.

Reading Spanish

You know more than you think!

As you can see, some common Spanish words are exactly the same as our own and so don't present any difficulty at all.

Nor do words we have taken from Spanish and which have passed into everyday use. For example, *patio, siesta, fiesta.*

Can you think of any more of these borrowed words?

Next, there are a large number of words which are **nearly** the same in Spanish as in English, and so are still easy to recognise.

If you see a word with an 'f' in it in Spanish, try changing the 'f' to 'ph' to make an English word. It doesn't always work, of course, but it's worth a try.

So, if you saw *física* written on a school timetable, which school subject would it be?

And what are you being warned about at the bottom of this entrance ticket?

!GLESIA DE SANTO TOME
Imperial Ciudad de Toledo

VALE para la visita al Cuadro del Greco, «El Entierro del Conde de Orgaz» (SIGLO XVI)

PROHIBIDO HACER FOTOGRAFIAS

Similarly, if a Spanish word begins with 'es', try taking off the 'e':

What do you think *especialidad* means?

Restaurante
L'Albufera

ESPECIALIDAD EN ARROCES

And what about *esquí*?
(Remember 'qu' is a 'k'
sound in Spanish)

As a general rule, always **say** the word to yourself (with
the right Spanish pronunciation!). The sound can
sometimes make the meaning clearer than just seeing the
word written down.

Warning!

Occasionally, words that look like English don't always
mean exactly the same thing. For example, *camping* and
caravaning are commonly used to mean a 'campsite' and
'caravan site'.

**CAMPING
CARAVANING
EL TORO BRAVO**

And just occasionally, words can be positively misleading:

It's not 'coaches without a conductor' for hire here, but
'self-drive cars'!

For practice . . .

Words taken or adapted from English are particularly common in certain areas – sport, for example

Estalló en el Chamartín-Master

Probable escándalo en la Liga juvenil

GOLF

Masters de Australia

Tres líderes en la primera jornada

SESTAO-CELTA **Día del club**

Con el récord en los talones

Excelentes exhibiciones de Abascal, González y Moracho

La maldición de los penaltis

1ª DIVISION

Con nueve goles; máximo realizador del equipo

These six headlines come from the sports section of a Spanish newspaper:

1 Which 'sports' words can you recognise?

2 Which other, more general, words can you understand because of their closeness to English?

Using the clues . . .

Even when you've never seen a Spanish word before, it's sometimes possible to work out what it must mean because of the context.

Imagine that you're at a Spanish station. It's one of those occasions when you need to sort things out quickly: finding the right platform or checking the time of a train, for example. You see this sign . . .

acceso is easy enough to guess and *paso* and *inferior* are close enough to English words for the meaning to be clear (especially with the help of the symbol), so, what must *vías* mean here?

Still on the station, you see this in the distance . . .

Sometimes the way to work out what a word means is to see if it contains any other words you know. This one starts with *Hora* . . . so, what does it mean?

This next one is not so easy.

You have already worked out what *vías* must be, and *cercanías* starts with *cerca*, which you probably know. So, what are you being directed to?
(Were you right? See the bottom of the page.)

For practice

You're walking down a Spanish street and see these two posters:

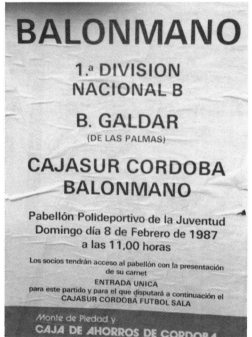

1   Can you work out what *balonmano* and *baloncesto* mean?

2   How many other words are similar to English ones?

(Platforms for local/suburban lines (i.e. places that are near))

Finally . . .

Here is a selection of signs, notices, newspaper headlines, etc. See how much you can understand, then discuss them with your teacher.

Islandia

Violenta erupción volcánica

Asistieron cerca de 40.000 espectadores

LA OPERA "OTELLO" REPRESENTADA EN UN ESTADIO DE FUTBOL

ESTUDIOS Y APARTAMENTOS

PRECIOS

		MAYO	JUNIO
ESTUDIO PARA:	1 Persona	1.250	1.875
	2 Personas	2.000	3.000
	3 Personas	2.750	4.125
APARTAMENTOS	4 Personas	4.000	6.000
	5 Personas	4.750	7.125
	6 Personas	5.000	8.000

NOTA: Estos precios se entienden por día y p

HELADOS LA JIJONENCA

HELADOS
GLACE
EIS
ICE CREAM

HORCHATA de CHUFA

HELADOS DE:
VAINILLA
FRESA
FRUTA
CHOCOLATE
MOKA
AVELLANA
TURRON
LIMON
NATA
CARAMELO
PLATANO
PISTACHE
TRUFA

El Gobierno francés concede la extradición a España de tres terroristas de ETA

Escuela Española de Esquí

Now read on . . .!

1

Hotels

When you go to Spain on holiday you may well be staying in a hotel and you'll want to be able to pick one that has the right facilities (is there a swimming pool? tennis courts?). Even if you aren't going yourself, you may still be able to help a friend or neighbour who doesn't understand Spanish.

Once you're there, it will make your stay easier and all the more enjoyable if you can understand how the system works: the laundry service, for example, and how to order breakfast in your room . . . without being woken up too early!

Finally, just to be on the safe side, you'd better know what you should do if there's a fire.

Breakfast arrangements

You have arrived with your sister at a hotel in Spain and are given room 16. The journey was tiring so you decide you will sleep in as late as possible next morning (Aug. 23) and then have breakfast in your room. Complete all the details on this form, which has to be hung on the outside of your door. (Your sister has decided on coffee and an omelette, while you have chosen tea and boiled eggs.)

HOTEL ◯ **ORIENTE**

Horario de desayunos 8,00–10,00

Fecha . . . . . N.º habitación . . . . . N.º de personas . . . . .

Deseo me sirvan el desayuno entre

8,00–8,15 [ ]   8,30–8,45 [ ]   9,00–9,15 [ ]   9,30–9,45 [ ]

8,15–8,30 [ ]   8,45–9,00 [ ]   9,15–9,30 [ ]   9,45–10,00 [ ]

Desayuno continental

Café [ ]   Nescafé [ ]   Té [ ]   Chocolate [ ]

Incluyendo:

Jugo de naranja, bollería, mantequilla y mermelada

EXTRAS

Huevos fritos jamón [ ]   Huevos fritos bacon [ ]

Tortilla francesa [ ]   Huevos pasados por agua [ ]

(. . . . . minutos)

Al hotel « don Paco »

A At reception one of the things you are handed is this little card, courtesy of the hotel. At first sight it looks the same both sides . . .

PL. JERONIMO DE CORDOBA, 4-5
TELEX. 72 3 32
TELEFONO 22 49 31
SEVILLA

hotel don PACO

COSAS QUE TENGO QUE HACER HOY

1
2
3
4
5

PL. JERONIMO DE CORDOBA, 4-5
TELEX. 72 3 32
TELEFONO 22 49 31
SEVILLA

hotel don PACO

COSAS QUE TENGO QUE HACER MAÑANA

1
2
3
4
5

1 What is it for?

2 How does the second side differ from the first?

B In your room you find a large white plastic bag:

1 What is it for?

2 Who should you hand it to?

3 What does *lavar y planchar* mean?

4 What must be filled in on the bottom line?

SERVICIO DE LAVADO Y PLANCHADO

ROGAMOS ENTREGUEN LA BOLSA A LA CAMARERA. GRACIAS

☐ **LAVAR Y PLANCHAR**

☐ **PLANCHAR**

☐ **LAVAR SOLAMENTE**

HABITACION Nº . . . .

C At breakfast there is a selection of packets of sugar with messages on them:

1 What does *gracias por su visita* mean?

2 . . . and *Le esperamos nuevamente*?

Hotel LOS CLAVELES

A neighbour is trying to choose a hotel for a Spanish holiday and has been sent these details:

Hotel LOS CLAVELES

150 habitaciones decoradas con lujo exquisito, todas con baño, teléfono y terraza privada. Aire acondicionado independiente en cada habitación. Piscina climatizada (en invierno). Pista de tenis con iluminación nocturna. El hotel está situado a sólo 75 metros de la playa. En el elegante comedor podrá disfrutar de una cocina internacional. Garaje. Jardín infantil. Peluquería de señoras. Coches de alquiler.

She has various questions in mind: can you help answer them?

Put a √ if the answer is 'yes'
 × if it's 'no'
 ? if the information isn't given

1 Do all the rooms have a bathroom?
2 Will I have to share a terrace?
3 Is there a lift?
4 Are the bedrooms air-conditioned?
5 Is there a swimming pool?
6 Will I have far to walk to the beach?
7 Do they have a car hire service?
8 Is there a ladies hairdressing salon in the hotel?
9 . . . and are there shops?

Tarjeta de Identidad

On arriving at your hotel, you are given this card at the reception desk:

TARJETA DE IDENTIDAD

| NOMBRE | HABITACION/PRECIO |

| LLEGADA   SALIDA | FIRMA |

La dirección y el personal del hotel le desean una feliz y agradable estancia.

GRACIAS POR SU VISITA

---

1 What has to be written in each of the four boxes?

2 What is the message from the hotel management and staff?

When you turn the card over, this is what you see:

MUY IMPORTANTE:

1 Rogamos a nuestros distinguidos clientes, que para evitar posibles errores al hacer uso del Bar o Restaurante, exhiban la presente tarjeta.

2 La dirección del hotel no responde de los objetos y valores no depositados bajo su custodia, contra recibo.

3 Se ruega dejen las habitaciones libres antes de las 12 horas.

---

3 When are you asked to show this card?

4 What won't the hotel accept responsibility for?

5 What are you asked to do in section 3?

17

'Sentimos comunicarle . . .'

A friend will be driving through Spain to a holiday resort and wants to spend a night in a hotel on the way. He has written to book a room and receives this reply. As he doesn't understand much Spanish, can you help work out what it says?

Hotel Plaza

Muy Sr. nuestro:

        Sentimos comunicarle que nos es imposible acceder a la reserva que solicita para el día 21 de Julio, ya que tenemos todo completo con anterioridad.

        En espera de poderle servir en otra ocasión, le saluda atentamente

---

1   What is said about his request?

2   Why is this?

3   What does the hotel hope?

Paradores

As well as many privately-owned hotels, Spain has a chain of excellent state-run *Paradores*. They are either newly built, taking advantage of good positions and excellent views, or are interesting old buildings – converted castles, for example, as shown on their logo.

In publicity brochures *Paradores* are listed with symbols beside the town and beside the hotel giving details about the facilities. To understand these symbols, you must look at the explanations given in the front of the brochure.

A Firstly, the symbols about the hotels themselves . . .

Signos Convencionales Relativos al Establecimiento

☎ Teléfono	⛊ Edificio histórico
♟ Bar	⌇⌇ Calefacción central
$ Cambio de moneda	⌂ Tiendas
⊠ Ascensor	⌀ Piscina
⚹ Sitio pintoresco	✦ Jardín
• Sitio céntrico	～ Playa
⊏⊐ Aire acondicionado en habitaciones	⥮ Altura sobre el nivel del mar

Draw the symbol which shows a *Parador* has a

1 garden
2 beach
3 swimming pool
4 lift
5 central heating system
6 shop

B Here are the symbols about the town:

Signos Convencionales Relativos a la Población

⊠ Correos	⋔ Ciudad monumental
☎ Teléfono	☐ Museos
$ Cambio de moneda	◯ Plaza de toros
⛉ Playa cercana	⛰ Deportes de montaña
⛄ Caza	⋕⋕⋕ Ferrocarril
⤙ Pesca	✈ Aeropuerto
⚠ Deportes náuticos	⛴ Puerto

What do these symbols tell you about the town's facilities?

1 ☐
2 ⊠
3 ◯
4 ⛴
5 ⋕⋕⋕
6 $

C Here are the details about three *Paradores* from a brochure:

---

① **Avila** ✉ ☎ $ ⋎ ⌇ 🏠 ☐ ○ ⛰

Parador Nacional « Raimundo de Borgoña »

A 64 Km. de Segovia, 98 de Salamanca y 113 de Madrid. Teléfonos: 918/21 13 40 y 21 27 46.

● ⋎ ♉ ✦ ⌇ ☎ ⊠ $ ⊥ 1.127m

② **Córdoba** ✉ ☎ $ ⋎ ⌇ 🏠 ☐ ○ ▥ ✈

Parador Nacional « La Arruzafa »

A 402 Km. de Madrid, 182 de Málaga y 241 de Huelva. Teléfono: 957/27 59 00.

⚘ ⊠ ⋎ $ ⌒ ✦ ⌂ ▭ ⌇ ☎ ⊥ 172m

③ **Ribadeo (Lugo)** ✉ ☎ $ △ ⋎ ⌇ ⛵ ⛴

Parador Nacional de Ribadeo

A 107 Km. de Lugo, 154 de La Coruña y 610 de Madrid. Teléfono: 982/11 08 25

⚘ ⋎ $ ✦ ⌇ ☎ ⊠ ⊥ 40m

---

1 Which *Parador* is nearest to Madrid?

2 Which *Parador* or *Paradores* would you choose if you wanted to
a get there by plane
b practise water sports
c see historic monuments
d have a beach nearby
e go fishing
f go climbing
g be in a picturesque spot
h stay in a historic building
i have an air conditioned bedroom
j be in a central position?

3 Which *Parador* is nearest to sea-level?

En caso de incendio

More regulations! Fixed to the door inside your hotel room you find these instructions about what to do in case of fire.

Even though they look rather complicated, you'd better sort out the main points . . .

EN CASO DE INCENDIO

● **SI DESCUBRE UN INCENDIO:**

- Comunique rápidamente a RECEPCION la situación del fuego
- Mantenga la calma: no grite ni corra
- Abandone su habitación, CERRANDO la puerta. La escalera mas próxima se halla a 4 m. a la izquierda. Otra salida posible se encuentra a 39 m. a la derecha
- No utilice los ascensores

● **SI LAS SALIDAS ESTAN BLOQUEADAS:**

- Permanezca en la habitación, colocando ropas húmedas en las ranuras de las puertas.
- Hágase ver por la ventana

---

1 If you discover a fire, who should you inform?

2 What's one thing you **shouldn't** do?

3 As you leave your room, what should you do?

4 Where is the nearest staircase?

5 . . . and where's another possible exit?

6 What are you told **not** to use?

7 If the exits are blocked, what is one of the things you should do?

Shopping

When in Spain, you'll certainly want to do some shopping . . . but what do all those notices on the doors mean? ('Closed'? 'No admittance'? 'Exit'?). And does that shop stay open or shut at lunch time?

Then, how about the publicity leaflets and posters? Are they announcing special offers, and if so, exactly what is on offer?

And when it comes to buying presents, will you be able to sort out which floor to go to in a big department store? This section will give you practice in recognising key words in situations like these.

Doors

Spanish doors, like those in this country, often have notices on them. Here are six examples: what do they mean?

1

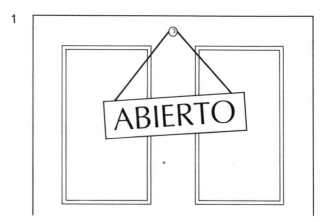

ABIERTO

2

Para mayor comodidad de nuestros clientes, no cerramos a mediodía.

3
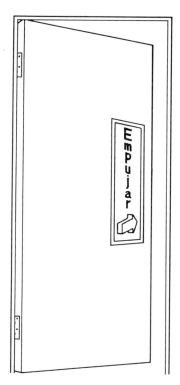

4
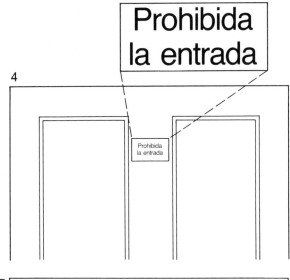

5
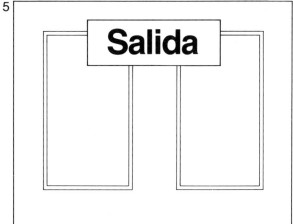

6
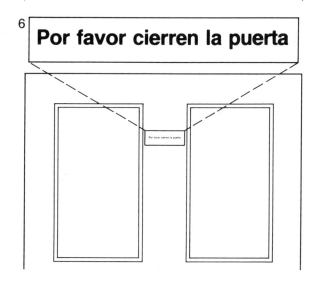

What's that?

Four tourists walking down a Spanish street see this building and each guesses what it might be. Who is right?

Publicity leaflets

A Walking down the street of a Spanish town, you are handed this leaflet:

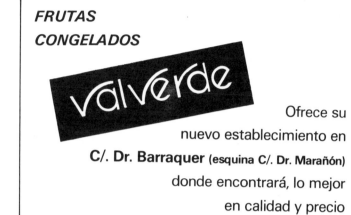

FRUTAS

CONGELADOS

Ofrece su

nuevo establecimiento en

C/. Dr. Barraquer (esquina C/. Dr. Marañón)

donde encontrará, lo mejor

en calidad y precio

1 What does the shop sell?

2 Where exactly in Dr. Barraquer street is it?

3 According to the leaflet, what will you find there?

B Later, you are given this card:

50 por 100.

PELUQUEROS **de Descuento**

MARTES DEL COLOR

Todos los MARTES, el 50 por 100 de
Descuento en todos los servicios de
Color. Tintes, Mechas, Pach, etc.

HASTA EL 31 DE DICIEMBRE

BLASCO DE GARAY, 70
TELEFONO 446 24 20

1 What kind of shop is the publicity for?

2 How much is the special offer worth?

3 When can you take advantage of it?

4 How long does it last?

5 What service is being offered?

Where can I buy . . . ?

This is the kind of thing you will see on Spanish shops:

Which shop would you go to (A–F) in order to buy . . .

1   a train ticket

2   a tube of insect repellent

3   some fish for dinner

4   some cakes for tea

5   a newspaper

6   a bracelet for your sister

Dévora

Look at this publicity leaflet for a shop:

SOMOS LA TIENDA QUE VD. BUSCA

Tenemos todos los estilos - TODAS LAS TALLAS

clásico y   vestir · juvenil sport

La mejor colección
de abrigos

VISITENOS, LE ENCANTARA

ESTAMOS EN:

PLAZA SAN ANDRES (detrás Iglesia San Andrés)

TELEF. 254 45 79

¡¡ *SU TIENDA AMIGA* !!

1   What kind of shop is it?

2   Where is it?

3   It claims to have *todos los estilos*. What does this mean?

4   . . . . and what about *todas las tallas*?

5   It says it has the best collection of . . . what?

6   If you were writing a similar leaflet for an English shop, what would you put for
    a ¡¡*su tienda amiga*!!
    b *Somos la tienda que Vd. busca*
    c *Visítenos, le encantará*

¡Grandes oportunidades!

Walking along the street of a Spanish town, you see this poster in the window of a shop

ESTA SEMANA

Grandes Rebajas en

Fíjese en algunos de nuestros precios

-CAMISAS _____ A *1.895,-Ptas.*

-PANTALONES CABALLERO _____ A *1.995,-Ptas.*

-PANTALONES VAQUEROS _____ A *2.595,-Ptas.*

-BLUSAS SRA. Y JOVENCITA _____ A *1.795,-Ptas.*

-VESTIDOS SRA. TODAS LAS TALLAS __ DESDE *1.995,-Ptas.*

-POLOS NIÑOS _____ A *795,-Ptas.* (DOS POR 1.400,-Ptas.)

¡Visítenos y Compruebe Precios!

Aceptamos todas las tarjetas de crédito

quien calcula compra en

---

1 What is the poster announcing?

2 When is it happening?

3 How much does a lady's blouse cost?

4 . . . and a man's pair of trousers?

5 What is the most expensive item on the list?

6 If you bought two polo-necked sweaters for your young brother, how much would you have to pay?

7 What does 'VESTIDOS SRA.' mean?

8 . . . and 'DESDE 1.995,-Ptas.?

9 What are you urged to do?

10 What is said about payment?

En 'El Corte Inglés'

You have a couple of hours to spend in 'El Corte Inglés', a large store. As there are a lot of things you want to do, this department directory will be useful . . .

GUIA DE DEPARTAMENTOS

Aparcamiento

Supermercado

Plantas
Flores
Cambio de moneda extranjera
Objetos perdidos
Animales

Perfumería
Bolsos
Librería
Discos
Instrumentos Musicales

Toallas
Ropa de cama y mesa
Lámparas
Muebles
Artículos de Viaje

Caballeros: Camisería
Confección
Ropa Interior
Zapatería Caballero
Paraguas
Regalos

Señoras: Confección
Medias
Punto
Complementos de Moda
Boutiques Internacionales
Juguetes

Bicicletas
Accesorios Automóvil
Peluquería de Señoras
Caballeros y Niños
Zapatería deportiva
Lista de Bodas

Agencia de Viajes
Cafetería-Restaurante
Estudio Fotográfico

1 You've made a list of what you need to do. Which floor do you have to go to for each item?

2 You've still got ten minutes left so you decide to go up to the second floor. What are three of the things on sale there?

3 Now it's time to meet your Spanish friend Elena in the café. Which floor do you go to?

4 Elena thinks she must have dropped some keys in the lift. Where is the lost property office?

1. Flowers for Elena's mother
2. Look at records
3. Haircut
4. Bottle of scent for Mother
5. Toy for Jackie
6. Change money
7. Look at sports shoes
8. Get extra suitcase for going home!

5 Now you must both join Elena's mother in the store car park. Whereabouts is it?

6 On the way there you see this keyring – just the thing for your brother who collects them. But maybe you should work out exactly what's written on it first . . .

Aquí vive el más guapo, el más listo, el más grande, el más simpático, el mejor...
el más modesto

Travelling around

When you're travelling in Spain by train or car, or even just finding your way round a town, you'll want to arrive at the right place without wasting time or getting lost.

Also, it's always as well to be quite clear about arrangements, whether you're meeting a visitor coming to stay with you or going to a Spanish friend's home for a party.

Horario de trenes

You are on holiday near Valencia and will need to get about by train. You see these details of local services in the paper . . .

HORARIO DE TRENES

Servicio Valencia-Torrent
A partir de las 5.15 y hasta las 21.45, un tren cada 15 minutos. Ultimo tren sale a las 22.15.

Servicio Torrent-Valencia
Desde las 5.48 hasta las 22.48 horas, ques es el último, cada 15 minutos.

Servicio Valencia-Villanueva de Castellón
A partir de las 6.15 cada hora, hasta las 20.15. Especial a las 21.15, que sólo llega hasta l'Alcúdia.

1   At what time in the morning does the service from Valencia to Torrent start?

2   When does the last train for Torrent leave Valencia?

3   How often is there a train back from Torrent to Valencia?

4   How often do trains normally run between Valencia and Villanueva de Castellón?

5   At what time does the last train going all the way to Villanueva de Castellón leave Valencia?

Tickets please!

1. Look at these three tickets. What type of transport do you associate with each?

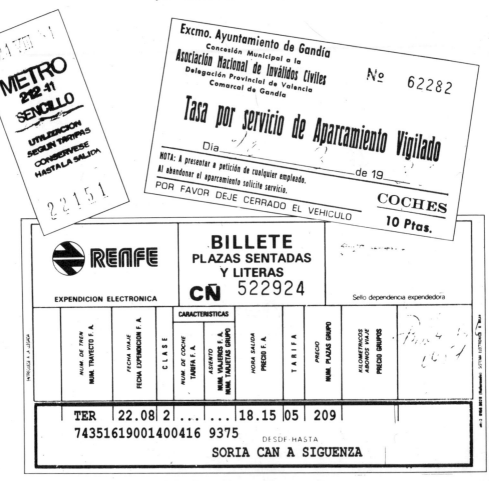

2. Was ticket A used for a single or a return journey?

3. ... and what does *'CONSERVESE HASTA LA SALIDA'* mean?

4. What service was offered for the 10 Ptas charge shown on ticket B?

5. ... and what does *'POR FAVOR DEJE CERRADO EL VEHICULO'* mean?

6. What town was the traveller going to with ticket C?

7. How much did the journey cost?

8. At what time did it start?

9. ... and on what date?

Travel arrangements

You have been expecting to hear from your Spanish
penfriend who is coming to stay with your family. This
card arrives from him . . .

¡Hola!

Espero que al recibo de esta postal os
encontréis todos bien, nosotros estamos
bien. Te escribo esta postal para decir-
te el día y la hora en que llegaré a
Englaterra. Salida de Valencia el 11 de
Julio a las 19 horas y llegada a Inglaterra a las 20'20 horas. En el vuelo
nº IB614
Dale recuerdos a tu familia
      Hasta pronto
        Eduardo
P.D. Te llamaré por teléfono antes de ira Inglaterra

Tell your parents what you can about the following:

1 Arrival date

2 Arrival time

3 Means of travel

4 Any message for them

5 Further relevant details

En la ciudad

You are staying in a Spanish town and need to find your way around. Luckily, you have a plan of the town centre.

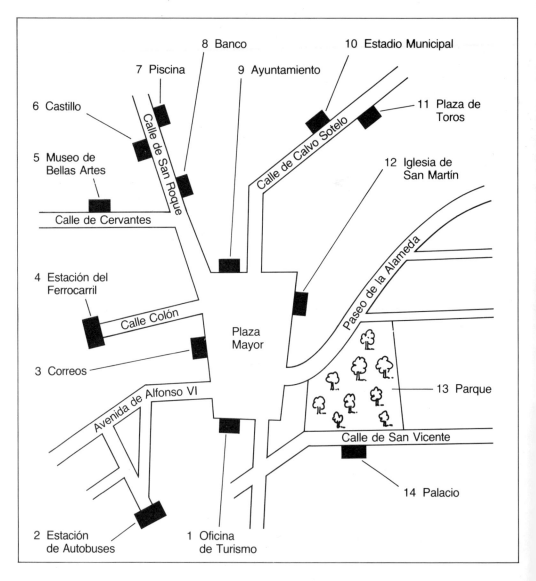

A Where would you go (write the number) if you wanted to

1 change some money?

2 buy some stamps?

3 watch a football match?

4 buy a train ticket?

B   What is the

1   Oficina de Turismo?

2   Iglesia de San Martín?

3   Castillo?

4   Ayuntamiento?

C   In what street is

1   the Palace?

2   the Art Museum?

3   the bullring?

4   the swimming pool?

D   During your stay you become friendly with a young Spaniard who invites you to come to a party at his family's flat and sends you these instructions to help you find your way.

Baja del autobús en la Estación de Autobuses y toma en seguida la primera calle a la derecha. Al llegar a la Avenida de Alfonso VI, tuerce a la derecha y sigue todo recto hasta la Plaza Mayor. Cruza la plaza y toma el Paseo de la Alameda que está enfrente. Baja por esta calle y verás el parque a mano derecha. Entonces, hay una pequeña calle a la derecha, al lado del parque. Mi piso está a la izquierda, exactamente enfrente de esta pequeña calle.

Using the town plan and his instructions, draw yourself a rough (but accurate!) sketch map showing the route to his flat and marking its exact position with an X.

Servicio Directo por Carretera

According to the leaflet,

1 What are two of the features of this service?

2 Apart from all over Spain, where else does it take you?

3 What form of transport is used?

4 . . . and what are two of the amenities it offers?

5 The routes are designed to connect with which forms of transport?

RENFE, Spain's rail network, also has another transport service, as described in this publicity leaflet . . .

. . . Un servicio rápido, eficaz y económico. Para viajar por toda España y buena parte de Europa. En modernos autocares que disponen de todas las comodidades (aire acondicionado, vídeo, suspensión neumática integral, etc.) y que ofrecen la mayor seguridad en ruta.

Además, las líneas de carretera de RENFE están especialmente estudiadas para servir de enlace con otras líneas de autobuses, con los recorridos de tren, etc. . .

RENFE
AREA DE TRANSPORTES POR CARRETERA

Autopista del Mediterráneo

You're touring by car in Spain and tomorrow you'll be taking the motorway south from Tarragona along the coast. You decide to have a look at the leaflet about the route. . .

A If you want to stop for the night, you have a choice of two hotels:

1 How many people can the Hostal La Ribera accommodate?

2 What chance do you have of getting a single room there? Why?

3 How many double rooms are there at the Hotel Residencia La Plana?

4 What three facilities does it offer?

Hoteles en la Autopista

AREA DE SERVICIO: La Ribera	Categoría	*
Hostal La Ribera	N.º Plazas	25
	H. Dobles	12
	H. Sencillas	1

Self Service · Aire Acondicionado *Telef. 964·310008*

AREA DE SERVICIO: La Plana	Categoría	***
Hotel Residencia La Plana	N.º Plazas	106
	H. Dobles	50
	H. Sencillas	6

Garaje · Aire Acondicionado · Parque Infantil *Telef·964·512550*

B

AREAS DE SERVICIO EN AUTOPISTAS

Donde encontrará:

* su cafetería
* su restaurante
* su tienda
* amplia zona de descanso
* aseos
* servicio telefónico

Y para su coche

* carburante y aceites
* accesorios y repuestos
* verificación gratuita de la presión de los neumáticos
* asistencia técnica

1 What are five of the services you can expect for yourself?

2 . . . and three of those for your car?

C

RECOMENDACIONES IMPORTANTES

★ Circule por la derecha

★ No se detenga jamás en un carril de circulación

★ En caso de condiciones meteorológicas adversas (niebla, nieve, lluvia, etc.) encienda las luces adecuadas y circule con precaución.

What three pieces of driving advice are you being given here?

D The leaflet also has brief notes about places near the motorway . . .

BENIDORM:

Capital turística de la Costa Blanca.
Ofrece dos grandes playas de finísima arena.
Cuenta con numerosas plazas hoteleras,
apartamentos, comercios, restaurantes. Su clima
atrae a numerosos visitantes durante todo el año.

What are three of the things it says about Benidorm?

37

4

At home

If your penfriend writes telling you about her new flat or a neighbour is considering buying property in Spain, it could be useful to know the words for the different rooms and facilities. This section will also help with pets, personal details, clothes and Christmas.

Lost and found

Looking through the newspaper at your penfriend's house you notice this . . .

Perdida perra pointer, zona Bravo Murillo/ Abascal, día 21. Pelo corto, blanca y canela. Responde por 'Tara'. Se gratificará. Teléfono 4485508

Encontrado perro cocker tres colores (negro, blanco, marrón). Lleva collar rojo. Teléfono 2614246

---

1 What has been lost?

2 . . . when?

3 Write down two pieces of information about it.

4 What does *se gratificará* mean?

5 What has been found?

6 What is said about its colour?

7 What other piece of information is given about it?

Apartamento, 3 dormitorios

A family friend is thinking of buying a flat in Spain and has received this publicity material . . .

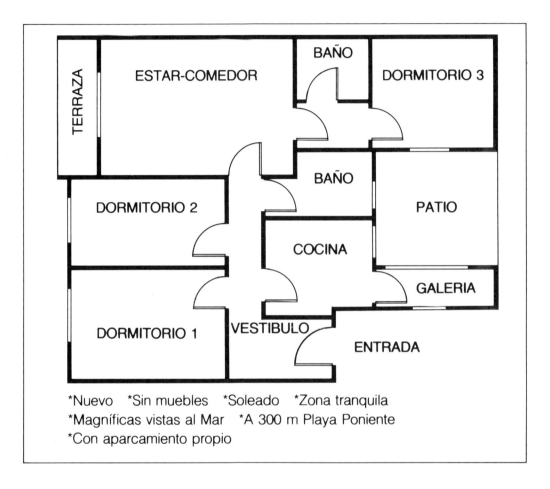

*Nuevo   *Sin muebles   *Soleado   *Zona tranquila
*Magníficas vistas al Mar   *A 300 m Playa Poniente
*Con aparcamiento propio

As she doesn't understand much Spanish, can you help her?

1   Roughly copy the plan and label it in English.

2   From the text underneath, she thinks that the flat is
    a new
    b fully-furnished
    c in a quiet position
    d near the centre
    Is she right? If not, give the correct version.

3   What else can you tell her about the flat? Write down as much additional information as you can.

Tu nueva amiga . . .

You have been given the address of a Spanish girl who
wants a penfriend and you sent off your first letter about a
month ago. This is the reply . . .

Granada 12 de marzo

Querida amiga:

Me alegro mucho que me hayas escrito. ¿Sabes?
He pensado que es mejor que te escriba en español y
tú me escribes en inglés, y luego, la próxima carta
yo te escribo en inglés y tú en español. ¿Quieres?

Respecto a tu español, para seis meses que lo
llevas dando, no está mal.

Tengo trece años. Mi cumpleaños es el 5 de julio.
Tengo una hermana de 16 años. Somos sólo dos
chicas. No tengo animales ahora, antes tenía un
perro pero le dimos a unos amigos.

Mi casa, bueno, vivo en un piso que tiene
cuatro habitaciones (el salón, un comedor y dos
dormitorios), la cocina y el cuarto de baño también.

Yo toco la guitarra y me gusta mucho la
música.

Espero que seamos buenas amigas. A ver si en
la próxima carta puedo enviarte una foto mía.
Tú envíame una tuya.

Sin más
tu nueva amiga
Lola

1   What arrangements about writing does Lola suggest?

2   What does she say about your Spanish?

3   How many of the following details about her can you fill in?
    a Age . . . . . .
    b Birthday . . . . . .
    c Brothers and sisters . . . .
    d Pets . . . . . .
    e House/flat . . . . . .
    f Rooms . . . . . .
    g Pastimes . . . . . .

4   At the end of her letter, what does she suggest you send each other?

Tintorería

Accidents can happen, so you may need some dry cleaning done when you're in Spain . . .

1   For what item(s) will the charge be
    a 275 pts.
    b 300 pts.
    c 325 pts.
    d 375 pts.?

2   How much will it cost you to have the following cleaned
    a a suit
    b an overcoat
    c a blanket
    d curtains?

3   What does *IVA INCLUIDO* mean?

TINTORERIA
LISTA DE PRECIOS
IVA INCLUIDO

Americana	375 pts.
Pantalón	300
Chaleco	250
Traje	675
Gabardina	675
Abrigo	675
Corbata	275
Jersey	325
Vestido liso	475
Falda lisa	325
Blusa a partir de	335
Cazadora a partir de	425
Chaquetón a partir de	550
Falda plisada a partir de	450
Mantas a partir de	695
Colchas a partir de	825
Visillos a partir de	200 metro cuadrado
Cortinas a partir de	295 metro cuadrado

Christmas

A Spanish boy explains to his penfriend what happens during the Christmas holidays.

Madrid, 10 de Enero

Querido amigo:

¿Qué tal has pasado tus vacaciones de Navidad? Yo me he divertido mucho, sobre todo el día 31 por la noche.

Aquí se celebra el día 24 por la noche, que se llama Nochebuena, el día 25 que es el día de Navidad y en mi familia vamos a comer a casa de los abuelos y nos reunimos con mis primos y tíos y tomamos turrón y mazapanes de postre. El día 31 por la noche es la fiesta de Nochevieja y es cuando más nos divertimos. Yo estuve esa noche en una fiesta hasta las 8 de la mañana del día 1. Ese día celebramos el Año Nuevo.

Luego la otra gran fiesta es el día 5 por la noche que es la noche de Reyes y luego el día 6 que es el día de Reyes, que es cuando se reciben los regalos.

Bueno, cuéntame algo de tus vacaciones y de tus estudios que espero que vayan bien, los míos regular.

Un abrazo:

Rafael

---

1 What does Rafael ask his penfriend?

2 During which part of Christmas Eve are there celebrations?

3 Where does Rafael's family go on Christmas Day?

4 Who else is there?

5 According to Rafael, which festivities during the holidays were the most enjoyable?

6 When did the party that Rafael went to finish?

7 What happens on January 6th?

8 What two things does Rafael ask his penfriend to tell him about?

Mi piso

As you hope to go and stay with your Spanish penfriend
Isabel next Easter, you have written asking about the
family flat. Her reply to your letter has just arrived. This is
the part which describes the rooms and where they
are . . .

Mi piso tiene siete habitaciones. Al entrar
hay un hall. Enfrente del hall está el
salón que tiene una pequeña terraza donde
mi familia y yo solemos pasar algunos
ratos en el verano. A la izquierda del
hall hay un pasillo y a cada lado del
pasillo están las distintas habitaciones.
La primera habitación a la derecha es
el cuarto de estar donde suelo pasar
algunos ratos con mi familia. Enfrente
del cuarto de estar está la cocina. La
segunda habitación a la derecha es el
comedor y enfrente del comedor está
la habitación de mi hermana la pequeña.
La tercera habitación a la derecha es
mi dormitorio donde suelo escuchar
música, leer libros y también hacer
mis tareas. Enfrente de mi habitación
está la habitación de mis padres y
al final del pasillo, entre mi habitación
y la habitación de mis padres, hay un
cuarto de baño.

1 Draw a sketch plan of the flat, labelling the rooms
   (in English) and showing where they are in relation to
   each other.

2 When is the terrace used?

3 What does Isabel say that she does in her room?

5

At school

Do Spanish children study the same subjects as you . . .
and do they spend more or less time at school each
week? What happens if they fail an exam? And what sort
of programme might be arranged if you went on an
exchange visit with a Spanish school?

Mucho que estudiar

1   Why hasn't Marisa written sooner?

2   What science subject does she study?

3   What are two things she says about English?

4   What is Marisa soon going to be doing?

5   Just before signing off, what does she ask Helen to do?

6   What does she say in the postcript?

Querida Helen

Perdóname por no haberte escrito antes pero es que en mi colegio hemos estado de exámenes y he tenido mucho que estudiar.

En mi colegio, que es un colegio de monjas, estudio matemáticas, historia, inglés, literatura, física, latín, gimnasia y otras asignaturas. Las que más me gustan son la física y el inglés. Llevo estudiando inglés cinco años y sé bastante.

Yo me voy a cambiar pronto de piso así es que cuando me escribas me pones esta dirección.

Avda. Almogávares, 58 – 2° – 2
14006
CORDOBA
ESPAÑA

Adiós Helen
Escribe pronto
tu amiga
Marisa

P.D. Saludos a tus padres y hermanos.

Evaluación

The following comments are taken from a list designed to help Spanish teachers assess their pupils:

1 Llega puntualmente a las clases

2 Participa activamente en los deportes

3 Su conducta por lo general es buena

4 Inconstante. Abandona fácilmente lo comenzado

5 Es popular entre los de su grupo

6 Con frecuencia olvida su equipo de deportes

7 Sus cosas están en perfecto orden

8 Demuestra poco interés en estudiar y aprender

9 Impide atender el resto de la clase

10 Con frecuencia llega tarde al colegio

Which one best fits . . .

a Andrés, who's the popular one in the group

b Blanqui, who's often late for school

c Conchi, who's
usually well-behaved

d David, whose locker
is always tidy

e Encarni, who's keen
on sport

f Felipe, who arrives
on time for lessons

g Gerardo, who couldn't care less about work

h Helena, who's always forgetting her games kit

i Isabel, who doesn't stick at what she's started

j José Luis, who distracts the rest from work

School routine

Here are some details from a booklet issued to pupils in a Valencian high school

A

CUADRO DE ASIGNATURAS Y HORAS SEMANALES

Asignaturas	Horas semanales
1 Lengua Española y Literatura	4
2 Lengua Extranjera (Francés o Inglés)	4
3 Dibujo	3
4 Música y Actividades Artístico-Culturales	2
5 Historia	4
6 Etica o Religión	2
7 Matemáticas	5
8 Ciencias Naturales	5
9 Educación Física y Deportiva	2
10 Valenciano	3

1 How many hours a week does Science have?

2 . . . and how many are given to Spanish?

3 Which foreign languages are taught?

4 Apart from Valencian, which subject has three hours a week?

5 . . . and which ones have two hours?

B

1 At what time does morning school end?

2 . . . and afternoon school begin?

3 How long is morning break?

4 What is the maximum number of teaching hours per afternoon?

5 What do the pupils do on Wednesday afternoons?

6 What does the underlined bit at the end say?

HORARIOS

El régimen horario será el siguiente:

ENTRADAS

Mañanas .... 8, 30 H.
Tardes .... 16 H.

SALIDAS

Mañanas .... 14 H.
Tardes .... 19 H.

Por las mañanas habrá un máximo de cinco horas lectivas para los alumnos, en jornada partida por media hora de recreo, de 10,30 H. a 11 H. Por la tarde el máximo será de tres horas lectivas. La tarde del Miércoles será libre para todos y dedicada a Actividades Extraescolares.
<u>Los alumnos deberán permanecer en el Centro en las horas que corresponden al presente horario . . .</u>

C

Which sports are played in the school?

DEPORTES

Se realiza todos los años un torneo deportivo en los deportes siguientes:

BALONMANO, BALONCESTO, BALONVOLEA, FUTBOL, TENIS, TENIS DE MESA, AJEDREZ

Intercambio

Your school has arranged an exchange visit with one in Córdoba. On arrival at Málaga airport, you're given a copy of the Spanish school's programme for your stay. This is the first part of it . . .

INTERCAMBIO CON GRAN BRETAÑA
Programa de estancia en Córdoba

Día 6 Viernes:
14.00 horas: Salida desde el Instituto para Málaga. Recepción de los estudiantes británicos en el Aeropuerto. Vuelta de Málaga: será aproximadamente entre las 12 y la 1 de la madrugada.

Día 7 Sábado:
Estancia en las respectivas familias.

Día 8 Domingo:
12.30: Comida en el campo de los Villares. Punto de encuentro el bar de los Villares. Pedimos a los padres que colaboren en el transporte de los chicos.

Día 9 Lunes:
8.30: Entrada al Instituto.
11.30: Reunión de todos los estudiantes del Intercambio con los profesores en la Sala de Juntas para comentar incidencias y posibles aclaraciones.

Día 10 Martes:
8.30: Salida para Sevilla desde el Instituto. Visita a la ciudad.
21.00: Llegada a Córdoba.

Día 11 Miércoles:
8.30: Jornada lectiva habitual.
11.30: Visita a la Ciudad, acompañados por un profesor del Centro. A las 14.00 horas los estudiantes españoles recogerán a los compañeros ingleses en la plaza de las Tendillas.

1. When are you expected to arrive in Córdoba from the airport?

2. Who will you be with on Saturday?

3. What is planned for Sunday?

4. Who is asked to help on this occasion and in what way?

5. Where will you be on Monday?

6. What is happening on Tuesday?

7. What is planned for 11.30 on Wednesday?

8. What should happen at 2.0 pm?

Retaking examinations

Salamanca 9 Septiembre

Querido Paul:

Me alegró mucho tu carta, la recibí ayer – ¿has visto que rápido soy para contestarte?

El pasado viernes yo estuve en tiempo de exámenes. Yo he tenido que recuperar tres asignaturas. Estoy contento porque he aprobado las tres. Casi todos mis amigos han aprobado y digo casi porque hay uno que ha suspendido y tendrá que repetir el 2º curso. ¡Qué pena!

¿Cómo te lo has pasado en vacaciones? Yo me lo he pasado muy bien.

No sé qué más contarte, me despido con un abrazo

Roberto

---

1. What was Roberto's reaction to having a letter from Paul?

2. When exactly did he receive it?

3. When did Roberto take some exams?

4. How many subjects did he have to retake?

5. What was the result?

6. How many of Roberto's friends failed?

7. What will the friend(s) have to do?

8. What reason does Roberto give for not making his letter any longer?

If you decide to eat in a restaurant or buy something from a take-away you'll need to understand the menu and price list. Also, if you're choosing a place to eat from the guide book, you'll want to sort out the type of meal it serves (traditional? Chinese? regional dishes?), when it's open and how to get there. And if you've rented a flat, how confident are you of understanding the instructions that go with the sandwich toaster, or the ones that tell you how to make up that delicious instant sweet?

Menú

1 What information, besides the address, is given to help you find the 'Estrella del Mar'?

2 When is the special 550 pts. menu available?

3 All four menus include *Pan, Vino o Cerveza*. What does this mean?

4 What are two of the desserts on offer?

5 ... and one type of fish mentioned?

6 What does *Platos para llevar* mean?

7 A barbecue is available in the evening. Whereabouts?

Restaurante

"Estrella del Mar"

Mare Nostrum, 3   (Detrás Hotel S. Luis)

PLAYA DE GANDIA

Menú especial todos los días por 550 pts.

I.V.A. INCLUIDO

Paella Valenciana	Fideua
Merluza Romana	Escalope
Fruta	Flan
Pan, Vino o Cerveza	Pan, Vino o Cerveza
Macarrones	Potaje o Judias Salteadas
Sardinas plancha o estofado	Lomo a la Plancha
Helado	Fruta en Almibar
Pan, Vino o Cerveza	Pan, Vino o Cerveza
Platos para llevar	Servicio Especial Noche
Paella o Fideua	Barbacoa Jardin
200 pesetas Ración	Pescados y Carnes espec.

Servicio Carta

Where to eat

A   You are staying in Gandía near Valencia. As it is nearly lunchtime you look at a menu in the window of a restaurant:

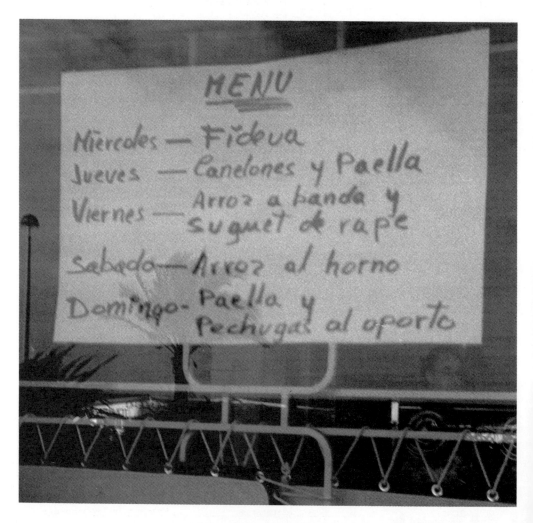

1   What days of the week **isn't** the restaurant open?

2   Rice is used a lot in this part of Spain. What is the word for 'rice' in the menu?

B Someone then hands you a leaflet for a rival establishment, the *Restaurante La paramunt*. This is what one side of the leaflet looks like

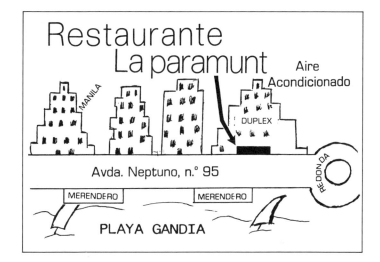

What do the following mean

1 Avda.

2 n.°

3 playa

4 aire acondicionado

C You turn the leaflet over . . .

1 What is Semana Santa?

2 What is on offer for 700 ptas.?

3 Who can do the same for 400 ptas.?

4 According to the leaflet, how many different dishes are available?

SEMANA SANTA

BUFFET LIBRE

La paramunt

Coma todo lo que quiera por **700 ptas.**

niños **400** ″

PIDANOS PRESUPUESTO PARA BANQUETES

DEGUSTE NUESTROS CUARENTA PLATOS DIFERENTES CON PAELLA, FIDEUA etc... etc...

Restaurantes

Before deciding where to eat, you'll want to find out about the style of food the restaurant serves, when it's open and exactly whereabouts it is.

1 What are three of the things on the menu at the *Barbacoa Alfredo*?

2 What style of cooking will you get at *Las Vegas*?

3 . . . at *El Dragón*?

4 . . . and at *Darío's*?

5 Which restaurant is closed on Mondays?

6 . . . and which is closed on Sundays?

7 . . . and which is open every day, Sundays included?

8 At what time does the *Barbacoa Alfredo* open on a Wednesday evening?

9 . . . and when does it close?

10 Which restaurant is open all summer?

11 What special directions are given to help you find
a *El Dragón*
b *Las Vegas*
c *Los Rosales*

12 Which restaurant has a private car park?

13 . . . and which one suggests where you can park?

14 Where can you get take-away meals?

15 . . . and where is there a disco?

16 What two things are you promised at *El Dragón*?

Restaurante
LAS VEGAS

COCINA ESPAÑOLA
PLATOS TIPICOS

ALEMANES 57 (FRENTE A LA CATEDRAL)
TELEFONO 24 41 35
CERRADO DOMINGOS

Restaurante Chino
EL DRAGON

- **Servicio impecable**
- **Precio razonable**
- **Comidas para llevar**

Tfno: 43 70 39

Santo Domingo de la Calzada, 20
(detrás Hotel Los Alamos)

darío's COCINA CASTELLANA

Joaquín María López, 38
Reservas: 43 18 25
(aparcamiento en Galileo, 71)

Comunica a sus clientes y
amigos, que permaneceremos
abierto todo el verano

LOS ROSALES

RESTAURANTE
BARBACOA
DISCOTECA

Castilleja de la Cuesta
(Autopista Sevilla-Huelva)

Aparcamiento privado

Abierto todos los días,

domingos y festivos
inclusive

BARBACOA ALFREDO
Bar-Restaurante

COSTILLAS DE CERDO
FILETES   POLLO
HAMBURGUESAS
HORARIO
DE MARTES A VIERNES:
de 13 a 16, 30 y de
20, 30 a 1 madrugada
SABADOS DOMINGOS
Y FESTIVOS:
de 14 a 17 y de 20, 30
a 1 madrugada
LUNES: CERRADO
SAN LUIS, 6 TELF. 423150

Al restaurante ≪ Casita ⫽ Príncipe ≫

As well as being your brother's birthday, it's the last evening of your Spanish holiday, so the family has decided on a meal out in a restaurant. Before going in, you have a good look at the menu.

𝕮𝖆𝖘𝖎𝖙𝖆 ⫽ 𝕻𝖗𝖎́𝖓𝖈𝖎𝖕𝖊

ENTRADAS

	ptas.
Entremeses "CASITA"	400
Sopa de la Casa	225
Consomé al Jerez	225
Ensalada Mixta	300
Ensalada	200
Jamón Serrano	600
Fabada Asturiana	400
Judías verdes con Jamón	450
Revueltos "PRINCIPE"	550
Huevos con Jamón	450

CARNES

	ptas.
Chuletas de Cerdo	500
» de Cordero	750
» de Ternera	750
Ternera Asada	650
Churrasco	975
Escalope Vienés	700
Cochinillo	975
Pollo Asado	500

PESCADOS

	ptas.
Bonito "Costa Brava"	700
Salmón con salsa Tártara	900
Lenguado al Gusto	850
Bacalao a la Vizcaína	700
Gambas al ajillo	600

POSTRES

	ptas.
Fruta del Tiempo	150
Flan	200
Helado Variado	200
Tarta Helada	275
Tarta de Whisky	300
Melocotón en Almíbar	250
Postre "CASITA"	425
Sorbetes: Manzana-Naranja-Limón	325

Natillas instantáneas

You're on a self-catering holiday in Spain and have bought a packet of dessert creams. Now to make them up: you look at the instructions on the back . . .

1 How many dessert creams can you make from this packet?

2 How long should it take to make them?

3 What is the first thing you are told to do?

4 What do you have to add to the contents of the packet?

5 What are you told **not** to do?

6 Once you have poured the desserts into dishes, what should you next do?

7 What suggestion is given at the bottom?

En un minuto cuatro natillas

Forma de preparación

Vaciar el contenido de la bolsa en un recipiente. Añadir tres cuartos de litro (750 c.c.) de leche

fría y mezclar hasta que el producto quede completamente diluido (no batir ni usar batidora eléctrica).

Servir en platos y dejar reposar en el frigorífico 15 minutos.

Sugerencia

Si desea natillas más líquidas utilice un litro de leche. Si desea natillas más espesas utilice solamente medio litro de leche.

---

1 What does *PESCADOS* mean?

2 . . . and what about *POSTRES*?

3 How much does soup cost?

4 . . . and ham and eggs?

5 What would you ask for if you wanted roast chicken?

6 . . . green beans and ham?

7 . . . prawns with garlic?

8 If you ordered *Melocotón en Almíbar*, what sort of fruit would you get?

9 Three different kinds of chop are on the menu. What are they?

10 . . . and what three flavours of sorbet?

11 If you ordered a mixed salad, salmon with tartare sauce and an ice cream, how much would it cost?

Unas vacaciones bien merecidas

You're in a holiday flat in Spain with your mother and brother. It would be nice to have a special celebration meal . . . but who's going to do all the cooking? A Spanish neighbour gives you this publicity leaflet and wonders if it will solve the problem.

SEÑORA:

No trabaje este verano

¡ Tenga unas vacaciones *bien* merecidas ¡

" EL BARROCO "

RESTAURANTE

NUMERO UNO EN COMIDAS SELECTAS, LE PREPARA **POR ENCARGO**

deliciosos platos, **listos para llevar.**

TLF. 890 04 33
C/ FLORIDABLANCA, 32

Encargos de 18:00 a 12:00 horas

A 1 What, according to the leaflet, is the lady of the house **not** to do?

2 . . . and what does she deserve?

3 How does the *El Barroco* restaurant rate itself?

4 If an order is placed, what will *El Barroco* prepare?

5 . . . and what is specially useful about this for you?

6 When do they accept orders?

B Their selection of food is on the other side of the leaflet

---

LISTA DE PLATOS PREPARADOS

Sugerencias	**Precios por ración**
Entradas en frío	
Ensaladilla rusa	250.00
El pate hecho en casa	350.00
Coctel de mariscos	400.00
Sopas y verduras	
Sopa de ajo castellana	200.00
Sopa de verduras	200.00
Pimientos fritos	300.00
Huevos	
Tortilla de patata	200.00
Pescados	
Merluza a la vasca	600.00
Salmón ahumado	800.00
Carnes	
Chuletillas de cordero	450.00
Pollo asado en su jugo	400.00
Filete de ternera	425.00
Postres	
Fresas con nata	250.00
Tarta helada	250.00
Ensalada de frutas	200.00
Flan	175.00
Tarta de limón	200.00

---

1 What does *Precios por ración* mean?

2 What's the cheapest item on the list?

3 ... and the most expensive?

4 Finally you all decide what to have:
   Your mother would like seafood cocktail, roast chicken and fruit salad;
   Your brother wants vegetable soup, Spanish omelette and strawberries and cream;
   And you fancy Russian salad, lamb chops and ice-cream gâteau.
   Write down the nine items (in Spanish!) ready for the *El Barroco* restaurant.

Sandwichera

The villa you've hired in Spain has an electric sandwich toaster as part of the kitchen equipment, and an instruction booklet with recipes as well . . .

A

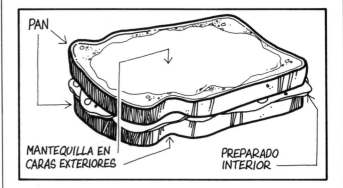

RECETARIO
COMPOSICION GENERAL DE UN SANDWICH

PAN

MANTEQUILLA EN CARAS EXTERIORES

PREPARADO INTERIOR

Sandwich 'MIXTO'

Pan – queso – jamón – queso – pan

Sandwich 'COLMENA' (Propio para niños)

Pan – queso – miel al gusto – queso – pan

Sandwich 'ITALIANA'

Pan – queso muy blando – trozos de champiñon cocido – tomate frito – aceitunas preferible negras – pan

1   What does MANTEQUILLA EN CARAS EXTERIORES mean?

2   In the Sandwich 'MIXTO', what goes between the two pieces of bread?

3   Who is the Sandwich 'COLMENA' designed for?

4   . . . and what does it have in the middle?

5   Describe what goes into the Sandwich 'ITALIANA' as fully as you can.

B But before starting to cook, it would be a good idea to look at the instructions and see what you should do . . .

POR FAVOR

Dedique unos minutos a la lectura de estas instrucciones . . .

INSTRUCCIONES DE USO

1   Conecte el aparato a la red, con la tapa en posición de cerrado. Al conectar se encenderá el piloto.
2   A los 7 minutos se apaga. Es entonces cuando la sandwichera está lista para cumplir su cometido.
3   Levante la tapa y disponga con cuidado para no quemarse los dos sandwiches en las cavidades.
4   Cierre la tapa sin oprimir demasiado para no deshacer los preparados.
5   A los 3 minutos, aproximadamente, los sandwiches están a punto para servir.

1   To start with, what position should the lid be in?

2   How long does the sandwich toaster take to warm up?

3   How do you know when it has warmed up?

4   When you put the sandwiches in, what are you told to be careful about?

5   . . . and what shouldn't you do when you close the lid?

6   How long will it be before the sandwiches are ready?

C Now for the not-so-nice part . . . cleaning up afterwards

LIMPIEZA

- Hágala siempre con el aparato des-conectado y aún caliente.
- Use un paño húmedo o esponja, simplemente con agua. Evite detergentes y también elementos abrasivos.
- Una vez fría la sandwichera, aplique otro paño muy limpio y seco.

NUNCA SUMERJA LA SANDWICHERA EN AGUA

---

1 What are you warned always to do?

2 What should you use to clean it?

3 When are you told to dry it?

4 What must you NEVER do?

7

Leisure

When you're in Spain you'll no doubt want to go to the cinema . . . but when does the film start and what does the write-up say it's about? This section will give you practice in recognising the kinds of words you'll need for various leisure time activities. And to begin with there's a horoscope to work out and, to end with, a puzzle to solve . . . just the kind of thing you'll find in a Spanish magazine.

Horóscopo

You're in Spain with a friend and see a horoscope in a magazine

ESCORPION (23 oct. a 22 nov.)
SALUD   B
TRABAJO   R
DINERO   B
AMOR   M

ACUARIO (20 en. a 18 feb.)
SALUD   R
TRABAJO   E
DINERO   R
AMOR   P

CLAVE DE SIGNOS
E = Excelente B = Bueno
R = Regular   M = Malo
P = Pésimo

1 What does the week have in store for your friend, whose birthday is 3rd November?

2 And if your own birthday was 26th January, what would you expect?

Los Juegos Olímpicos

Look at this chart showing when some of the events will be held:

BARCELONA 92

Calendario de las Competiciones

Julio							Agosto								
D	L	M	X	J	V	S	D	L	M	X	J	V	S	D	
26	27	28	29	30	31	1	2	3	4	5	6	7	8	9	
					√	√	√	√		√	√	√	√	√	Atletismo
√	√	√	√	√	√	√		√	√	√	√	√			Baloncesto
√	√	√	√	√	√	√	√	√	√		√				Balonmano
√	√	√	√	√	√	√	√	√	√	√	√		√		Boxeo
√			√	√	√	√	√		√						Ciclismo
	√		√		√		√		√	√	√	√		√	Equitación
√	√	√	√	√	√		√	√		√		√	√		Fútbol
√	√	√	√	√	√	√		√	√	√					Gimnasia
√	√	√			√	√	√								Natación
√	√	√	√	√	√	√	√								Tenis de mesa

1 What day of the week is 2 August?

2 . . . and 28 July?

3 When does the cycling start?

4 . . . and the table tennis end?

5 Which sports can you see on 8 August?

6 . . . and which can't you watch on 2 August?

7 Which competition begins on 27 July?

8 . . . and which one ends on 6 August?

¡El Teleski Náutico le espera!

This is an advertisement for cable water skiing at Benidorm

 **Teleski Náutico**

FACIL: En una hora, **cualquier persona** puede aprender a esquiar

SIN PELIGRO: Ni un solo accidente en veinte años

ECONOMICO: Porque pueden esquiar diez personas a la vez

EMOCIONANTE: Competiciones (58 kms/hora)

1 What does the advertisement claim that **anyone** can do?

2 What fact is given to show cable water skiing isn't dangerous?

3 Why is it inexpensive?

4 . . . and what can make it exciting?

Corrida de toros

This is a newspaper advertisement for a bullfight:

1 In which month will it take place?

2 . . . and at what time?

3 How many bulls will there be?

4 When are season tickets on sale in Victoria Street?

5 . . . and when can the general public buy tickets there?

6 If you wanted a ticket on the afternoon of the 19th, where would you go to get it?

PLAZA DE TOROS DE MADRID

DOMINGO, 19 DE AGOSTO, A LAS SIETE DE LA TARDE
Seis toros de El Sierro para
Marcelino Librero «EL MARCELINO»
PEPE PASTRANA
JOSE LARA
que confirma la alternativa
VENTA DE ABONOS: en calle Victoria, número 3. Viernes 17.
VENTA DE BILLETES AL PUBLICO: en calle Victoria, 3. Sábado 18 y domingo 19, mañana.
TAQUILLAS DE LA PLAZA DE TOROS: Sábado 18 y domingo 19.

A partir del lunes . . .

What's coming to the local cinema? You see this notice in the paper . . .

1 How much does a seat cost on Saturdays?

2 What is said about Wednesdays?

3 What is the film about? Write down three main points.

4 At what time does the last full programme start?

PRINCIPAL PALACIO Avda. de la Luz,59. Ptas. 350. Sábados y Festivos Ptas. 375. (cerrado los miércoles)

Jugando con la muerte (color)
Una banda internacional de traficantes de heroina y uranio usa España como base de operaciones. Agentes del país y norteamericanos se alían para combatirles (14)

Tarde 4.15 continua. Noche 10.20
Pases: 4.30, 6.20, 8.20 y 10.35

5 How many times is *Jugando la muerte* screened each day?

¡Diviértete!

Here are details about three different types of entertainment:

A

1   What type of entertainment is this?

2   Exactly where has it been set up?

3   What gets you in for only 200 Ptas.?

4   . . . and for what three days of the week is the offer valid?

B

> **JARDIN ZOOLOGICO.** Grandes mamíferos, aves y fieras. Ahora también gran exposición de las serpientes más venenosas del mundo. (Abierto desde las 10 h. hasta el anochecer, precios populares).

1   What place is this publicity for?

2   What exactly would you see in the big exhibition there?

3   What is said about opening hours?

C

RÍO SAFARI
DELFINARIO
ELCHE

El único safari de Europa visitado en barco

Río Safari Delfinario Elche es el lugar ideal para disfrutar de la naturaleza contemplando desde su embarcación: tigres, leones, monos, elefantes, rinocerontes, camellos, hipopótamos, etc. Río Safari, con sus seis mil palmeras adultas, crea un marco tropical único en su género. En la visita al delfinario se sentirá sorprendido por el gran espectáculo que ofrecen los delfines y focas en una hermosa piscina de 700.000 litros de agua.

1　In what form of transport do you visit this Safari Park?

2　Name seven types of animal you can see whilst doing this.

3　How many palm trees do they say there are?

4　Where exactly in the dolphinarium are the dolphins and seals?

A note from Ana . . .

. . . inside her Christmas card

Barcelona 15 de Diciembre

Querida amiga.

¿cómo estás? Espero que bien y que esta Navidad te traiga mucha felicidad y muchos regalitos.

No sé si te llegará con Tiempo este Christmas, es que no he podido escribirlo antes pues he estado muy ocupada preparando el Festival de Navidad del colegio.

¿Recibiste mi carta? ¿la que te escribí en Octubre? Por favor, escríbeme pronto y cuéntame muchas cosas.

Mis amigos y yo estamos empezando a hacer los preparativos para la fiesta de fin de año, por ahora Tenemos el local (en casa de Roberto) y el tocadiscos (de José), cada uno se encargará de comprar la comida, bebida etc...

Bueno, deseo que pases unas felices Fiestas en compañía de tu familia.

Te deseo esto con mucho cariño

Ana

---

1 What two things does Ana hope Christmas will bring you?

2 Why couldn't she write the Christmas card earlier?

3 What should you have received?

4 What does she ask you to do?

5 What are she and her friends getting ready for?

6 Where will it take place?

7 What is José contributing?

8 What will need to be bought?

Una fiesta

Barcelona 13 de Enero

Querida amiga,

¿cómo estás? yo muy bien, he pasado unas magníficas vacaciones de Navidad. Las he pasado en Barcelona con mi familia y amigos.

En mi carta de Navidad te conté que estábamos todos organizando una fiesta para fin de año, pues te diré que salió fenomenal, nos divertimos mucho, la fiesta terminó a las 6'30h de la madrugada, luego aún nos fuimos a un bar a tomar chocolate con churros, total, que nos acostamos todos a las 8h de la mañana. Ningún año nos quedamos tan tarde y a pesar de acabar tan cansada ya no pude dormir, simplemente me tumbé en la cama a descansar hasta las 3h de la tarde.

Contestando a tu pregunta, te diré que sí tenemos por costumbre en España recibir los regalos el 6 de Enero. Yo también he recibido discos este año y mis abuelitos me han dado dinero.

Escríbeme enseguida y cuéntame lo que has hecho durante tus vacaciones.

Muchos besos,

Ana

P.D. Recuerdos a tu familia y deseo que estén todos bien.

1 Which holidays is Ana writing about in her letter?

2 When did the party take place?

3 How did it go?

4 What happened
   a at 6.30 am
   b between 6.30 and 8 am
   c at 8 am
   d between 8 am and 3 pm

5 Which Spanish custom does Ana mention?

6 What present, apart from money, did Ana receive?

7 . . . and who gave her money?

8 At the end of the letter, what two things does she ask you to do?

9 . . . and what two things does she say in the 'P.S.'?

Puzzle: who's who?

Four people from different countries are lining up to go through Spanish customs. Can you sort out who's who, and their place in the queue?

Read the statements about them and fill in the grid (in English!)

1 El primero de la fila tiene veintiocho años y es médico.

2 El cuarto de la fila estará en España un año.

3 El francés está detrás del que tiene veintiocho años, y delante del que estará en España quince días.

4 El inglés está delante del alemán y no es profesor.

5 El médico es escocés y está delante del camarero.

6 El soldado está delante del alemán y tiene veinticinco años.

7 El escocés estará en España un mes y está delante del que tiene diecinueve años.

8 El profesor tiene treinta años.

9 El francés estará en España una semana.

	First	Second	Third	Fourth
Nationality				
Age				
How long will be in Spain				
Job				

Holidays

If you go to Spain for a holiday you may well need to understand campsite details (what to put on the booking form, the facilities available, rules and regulations), what to dial to phone home (or the local tourist office, the station . . .), and whether that sun tan cream you are about to buy really is the right one for you.

Llamadas internacionales

You're on holiday in Spain and need to phone home. You find these instructions in a tourist brochure:

● **Llamadas internacionales.** Para comunicar con otros países deberá marcarse: número 07 (acceso a la central internacional), indicativo del país, indicativo de la localidad y número del abonado. Los indicativos de los países europeos más comunes son: Alemania, R. F., 49; Austria, 43; Bélgica, 32; Francia, 33; Holanda, 31; Italia, 39; Portugal, 351, y Reino Unido, 44. Existen numerosas cabinas telefónicas en la calle desde las que se puede llamar utilizando monedas.

1 Which number do you dial first?

2 What is the code for the U.K.?

3 After dialling this code, what two things must you then dial?

4 What are you told in the last sentence?

En la plaza

You're touring in Spain with your family, and have stopped for a break in a small town. You go for a walk in the square where you see . . .

Prohibido tirar objetos a la fuente bajo multa de 1.000 pts.

What does the notice say?

Palacio de Viana

If you were on holiday in Córdoba and wanted to visit the Palacio de Viana it could be very annoying to get there . . . and then find it closed!

HORARIO

- **Invierno:**
  10,00 h. a 13,00 h. y de 16,00 h. a 18,00 h.
  Meses de Octubre a Mayo, ambos inclusive.
  Domingos y festivos de 10,00 h. a 14,00 h.

- **Verano:**
  9,00 h. a 14,00 h.
  Meses de Junio a Setiembre, ambos inclusive.

- **Cerrado los miércoles**

  Los espacios abiertos – 1 jardín y 12 patios – se visitan discrecionalmente. El interior, piso bajo y planta alta, en grupo, acompañados por guías que explican el contenido.

1 If you were on a winter break, at which of the following times could you get in?
   a 11 am, Monday 6 October
   b 5 pm, Sunday 23 November
   c 3 pm, Thursday 19 February
   d 1 pm, Sunday 12 April
   e 4 pm, Saturday, 10 May

2 And in summer, on which of the following occasions is it open?
   a 3 pm, Monday 15 June
   b 9 am, Sunday 5 July
   c 10 am, Wednesday 29 July
   d 1 pm, Tuesday 11 August
   e 1 pm, Saturday 26 September

3 a How many courtyards are there?
   b Which parts of the inside of the Palace can you go in?
   c What is one other thing that is said about visiting the inside of the Palace?

¡Hace mucho sol!

It's going to be another very hot day, so on your way to the beach you decide to get some sun tan lotion. But before buying it, it would be a good idea to read what is written on the label . . .

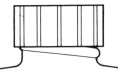

1 Who is it particularly for?

2 What are two examples of situations when it is specially recommended?

3 What two things are you told about putting it on?

4 Exactly how much protection does it claim to give?

Leche para el bronceado.
Alta protección: índice 6
Esta leche solar,* está destinada para las pieles sensibles al sol (tonos claros, piel de los niños), sol intenso (alta mar, nieve o montaña). Protege eficazmente contra el exceso de sol y permite un bronceado armonioso.
Aplicar uniformemente por todo el cuerpo y renovar con frecuencia la aplicación.

* índice 6 (Schulze): Permite permanecer al sol 6 veces más tiempo que sin protección.

Camping on the Costa Brava

You have decided to go camping, taking your tent, for a fortnight at Playa de Aro on the Costa Brava. Your stay there will start on the 1st. of August. Fill in this form to make your booking . . .

A

Por favor reserven una plaza para: Tienda ☐

Caravana ☐

Fecha de llegada _____

Fecha de salida _____

Dirección:

Nombre y apellidos _____

Calle _____   Ciudad _____

País _____   Fecha _____

Firma _____

B In the publicity brochure for the site you see these rules about arrival and departure:

> **Prohibida la entrada de coches a partir de medianoche.**
>
> **Recomendamos a los clientes que deseen emprender viaje a primeras horas del día, soliciten la factura el día anterior.**

1 What is forbidden after midnight?

2 If you want to set off early at the end of your stay, what must you do?

Alicante

A

¡Haga como el sol!

¡Pase el invierno en ALICANTE!

What are you urged to do on the cover of this tourist guide to Alicante?

B

A list of useful phone numbers is given in the guide. What number would you ring if you wanted to

1 report a robbery to the police

2 enquire about bus services

3 speak to the British Consul

4 ask the tourist office about local excursions

5 find out about car hire prices

6 ask the cost of a rail ticket to Murcia

7 call the fire brigade?

URGENCIAS Y SERVICIOS

Ambulancias	215117
Autobuses (estación de)	220700
Banco de Alicante	201299
Consulado Francia	266600
Consulado Inglaterra	216022
Consulado Alemania	217060
Bomberos	229080
Clínicas médicas	262322
Coches alquiler	206400
Farmacias	217860
Iglesia católica	212662
Oficina de Turismo	212285
Policía Municipal	284411
Renfe	226840
Reparación automóviles	222751
Taxis	200485

C This is part of the description of the town:

> Ciudad cosmopólita, alegre, elegante, con un magnífico puerto turístico y comercial y siete kilómetros de playas de arena y diez de rocas. Su clima mediterráneo, con temperaturas invernales de 18 a 22 grados y estivales de 26 a 30 grados, la hace ideal para las vacaciones. Cautiva al visitante por la luminosidad de su cielo y la hospitalidad de sus habitantes.

From this description, what are two of the things you learn about Alicante's

1 ''atmosphere''

2 port

3 beaches

4 climate?

Which campsite?

The family next door wants to spend a camping holiday in Spain and has sent away for details of three different sites. As they don't understand Spanish, they have asked you to help them sort things out.

1 Your neighbours are keen to know if certain facilities are provided. Copy the grid and tick the ones that are mentioned.

	Sited near the beach?	Facilities for children?	Sports facilities? Which?	Plenty of trees and shade?	Swimming pool?
CAMPING LAS DUNAS					
CLUB « LAS SALINAS »					
LA BALLENA ALEGRE					

	Shop?	Restaurant?	Electricity laid on?	Medical services?	Open all the year?
CAMPING LAS DUNAS					
CLUB « LAS SALINAS »					
LA BALLENA ALEGRE					

Camping Las Dunas

*Situado al borde del mar *Playa muy ancha de arena fina *Ideal para niños y la práctica de todos los deportes náuticos *Abundante vegetación en medio de una plantación de naranjos
*Supermercado, Bar y Restaurante *Abierto todo el año

CLUB « Las Salinas »

1ª. categoría. Situado en primera línea de mar, a 56 kms de Barcelona, con instalaciones de primera calidad y totalmente nuevas. Posee todos los servicios para la práctica de su deporte favorito (wind-surfing, tenis, etc.), tres piscinas (para adultos y niños), agua caliente gratis en los sanitarios, amplias parcelas de acampada de 70 m². con conexión eléctrica. Temperaturas medias junio, julio, agosto y septiembre 23°C.

LA BALLENA ALEGRE

A 9 minutos de Barcelona por autopista, « La Ballena Alegre » le invita a acampar en sus frondosos bosques y a bañarse en las transparentes aguas mediterráneas, disponiendo para ello de una hermosa finca, en la cual podrá situar su tienda a la sombra de los pinos en la misma playa. Este camping dispone de luz eléctrica, teléfono, bar, restaurante, supermercado, peluquería señoras y caballeros, duchas, WC, lavabos, asistencia médica y enfermería. Abierto todo el año.

2   Is any information given about the position of the campsites in relation to Barcelona? If so, what?

3   Write down one other facility offered by each site.

Skiing in Spain

Here are some extracts from a brochure about a short skiing course in the Pyrenees:

A

CURSILLO DE ESQUI

COMPRENDE:

- Alojamiento en hoteles y apartamentos de domingo noche a domingo siguiente mañana.

- 6 días de clases de esquí. Horarios: Lunes a viernes de 10 a 12 y de 14 a 16.
  Sábado de 10 a 12.

- Programa de actividades 'Après ski'.

1 What two types of accommodation are available?

2 . . . and for how many nights?

3 How many hours skiing tuition are there on a Wednesday?

4 . . . and on a Saturday?

B

NIÑOS HASTA 11 AÑOS –	REDUCCIÓN
Temporada Baja	700
Temporada Media	1.600
Temporada Alta	2.300
Fin de Año y Semana Santa	3.100

1 Who exactly can get a price reduction?

2 How much reduction do they get in Low Season?

3 . . . and in High Season?

4 At what two special times of year do they get a reduction of 3.100 ptas.?

C

Après Ski

Programa de actividades

Domingo

* Bienvenida
* Entrega dossier con detalle de
  actividades e información general

Lunes

* Comienzo del cursillo
* Proyección de películas de ski

Martes

* Iniciación campeonatos
* Gran fiesta infantil

Miércoles

* Cine comercial
* Concurso de baile

Jueves

* Proyección vídeo de clases de ski
* Bingo

Viernes

* Baile de disfraces
* Concurso de muñecos de nieve

Sábado

* Slalom cursillistas
* Entrega de trofeos y diplomas
* Cocktail de despedida

1 What does the 'dossier' handed out on Sunday contain?

2 What entertainment is there on Monday?

3 What is arranged for children on Tuesday?

4 When is there a dancing competition?

5 . . . and one for building snowmen?

6 Apart from Bingo, what is arranged for Thursday?

7 . . . and what are two of the things for Saturday?

Holiday news

Three Spanish girls have written to an English friend about their holidays:

A

... ¿Cómo pasaste tus vacaciones? Yo estuve en la playa en el mismo sitio del año pasado. Me lo pasé muy bien y me puse muy morena. Allí estuve un mes, Agosto, y luego en Septiembre me fui al pueblo de una amiga mía donde estaban las fiestas y me lo pasé fenomenal. Conocimos a un chico francés llamado Jérôme. Vive en Toulouse.

Besos y abrazos

María Teresa

B

LOS ALCAZARES
Paseo de la Concha

Hola Gill.
Te mando esta postal desde donde estoy pasando mis vacaciones de verano. Me lo estoy pasando muy bien y espero que tú también.
Aquí tengo muchos amigos con los que me voy a la playa y a las fiestas.
Ya te contaré más cosas cuando vuelva a Sevilla.
Escríbeme pronto
Besos
Mónica

Miss G Blake,
5 Church View,
Leatherhead,
Surrey,
Inglaterra

c

... Mis vacaciones las pasé en un pueblo de la sierra llamado San Rafael, es muy bonito, y me lo pasé muy bien Hacía mucho frío pero me he bañado en la piscina y también he ido a la disco- teca, pués me gusta mucho bailar.

Sin más, un abrazo y un beso

tu amiga

Isabel

1 Which girl says that she
   a . . . found the weather very cold
   b . . . wants her friend to write soon
   c . . . went to the swimming pool
   d . . . met a French boy
   e . . . has lots of friends there
   f . . . went to the disco
   g . . . went to the same seaside resort as last year

2 In which card or letter (write A, B or C) does the writer say she
   a . . . stayed in a pretty place
   b . . . hopes her friend is having a good time, too
   c . . . went to stay with a friend in September
   d . . . spent her holiday in a mountain village
   e . . . got very brown
   f . . . will tell her friend more when she gets back
   g . . . likes dancing very much

'Elementary, my dear Watson!'

Are you a good detective? Mr. X has been in Spain for several months and the items below were in his pockets. See how much you can find out about how he spent his time there.

1 On what day of the week did he go to a bullfight?

2 What time did it begin?

3 In what part of the town was the bullring?

4 What was Mr. X thinking about buying in Tarragona?

5 When did he have a meal in the Restaurante Coronada?

6 Which table did he sit at?

7 What sort of building did he pay 50 ptas. to visit in Segovia?

8 How did he travel between Torremolinos and Málaga?

9 What type of ticket did he buy?

10 On what date did he buy it?

11 When he went to *Playa del Bajondillo*, how did he get to the beach?

12 How much would it have cost to get there and back again?